THE INVISIBLE WORLD

The Invisible World

John Canaday

LOUISIANA STATE UNIVERSITY PRESS *Baton Rouge*

Copyright © 2002 by John Canaday
All rights reserved
Manufactured in the United States of America
First printing
11 10 09 08 07 06 05 04 03 02
5   4   3   2   1

Designer: Melanie O'Quinn Samaha
Typeface: Marigold and Galliard
Printer and binder: Thomson-Shore, Inc.

Library of Congress Cataloging-in-Publication Data

Canaday, John, 1961–
    The invisible world : poems / John Canaday
       p. cm.
    ISBN 0-8071-2775-2 (cloth : alk. paper) — ISBN 0-8071-2776-0 (pbk. : alk. paper)
    1. Middle East—Poetry. 2. Islamic countries—Poetry. I. Title.

PS3603.A524 I58 2002
811'6—dc21

                                                                          2001038990

Grateful acknowledgment is made to the editors of the following publications, in which some of these poems first appeared, sometimes in slightly different form: *The Beloit Poetry Journal:* "The Ninth Month," "Song of Myself"; *Bostonia Magazine:* "A Fast of God's Choosing," "Spring Cleaning"; *Harvard Review:* "New England Ghazal"; *Icarus:* "The Seventh Circle"; *The Massachusetts Review:* "The Invisible World"; *New England Review:* "The Empty Quarter," "The Snow Men"; *New Millennium Writings:* "Song of Myself"; *The Paris Review:* "A True Story"; *Poetry:* "Sheikh Majnoon"; *Raritan:* "Al Badr Street," "Exotic," "Impostors"; *Salamander:* "Third Person"; *Slate* (an internet journal): "Humid" (reprinted by permission).

"New England Ghazal" and "Spring Cleaning" were reprinted in the anthology *Contemporary Poetry of New England,* edited by Robert Pack and Jay Parini (University Press of New England, 2002). "New England Ghazal" was reprinted in *Ravishing DisUnities: Real Ghazals in English,* edited by Agha Shahid Ali (Wesleyan, 2000).

Thanks to Nicola Mason, editor at LSU Press.

The paper in this book meets the guidelines for permanence and durability of the Committee on Production Guidelines for Book Longevity of the Council on Library Resources. ∞

In memory of
Hussein bin Talal
and for
Noor al Hussein
and
Hamzah, Hashim, Iman, and Raiyah

I will venture to say thus much, That we are safe,
when we make just as much use of all Advice from
the invisible World, as God sends it for.

   —Cotton Mather, *Wonders of the Invisible World*

Their eyes have never looked into infinite space
Through the lattice-work of a nomad's comb.

   —W. H. Auden, "In Praise of Limestone"

Contents

THE INVISIBLE WORLD

Call to Prayer

The muezzin's prerecorded moan wells up
in dry darkness, flooding the air, garbled
by the playing of this same cassette again
and again, until it sounds like the wordless cry
of someone drowning. Here, one's sleep must be
full of the deaf dreams of the faithful.
"Is nothing sure but that God's mercies are
more numerous than all the desert's sands?"
A few last words bunch and scatter like swallows.
My body's salts taste foreign on my lips.
I wait a long while, barefoot on the cool
stone floor, until a rooster whoops and squawks
its morning prayer. Somewhere this side of Mecca,
the sun is rising even as I speak.

I. Entrée

Entrée

And then went down to the ship . . .
—Ezra Pound, Canto I

What punch-drunk duffer baked a ham entrée
to serve midway into a twenty-hour flight
to the Islamic Middle East? And on an Arab-
owned airline, no less! What chutzpah,
I think—though surely there's a better word.
No sign of cruel or comic forethought here:
rather, it seems a chain of circumstance,
abetted by a sleepy stewardess,
has led the roaming faithful into sin. I'm torn,
not knowing whether I should tell someone
about this breach of dietary law
or mind my own damn business for a change.
But what my business is is hard to say:
I'm on my way to spend a year in Jordan
tutoring the children of American
expats; and yet, of course, I'm in it for
the odyssey. Does that make me a tourist
or a resident of sorts? Meanwhile, as I
dither, my fellow passengers go on
devouring their chicken cordon bleu
with ardor an imam might advocate
for abstinence in Ramadan. (Thank God
it's not that holy month, or there'd be hell
to pay.) So: rein my native spirits in?
Or play the interfering foreigner?
Discretion dictates silence. Watch and learn.
But I'm no transparent eyeball: I see with
my eyes, not through them—*pace* Ralph and Bill.
And yet…I hesitate…then raise my hand,
uncertain as a kid who's new in class,
and punch the button for a stewardess.
A large man at my right hand finishes
his dinner, sees me looking, wipes his lips,
and smiles. A trim-coifed stewardess arrives.

I point down at my tray—"I think this stuff
is ham," I stutter, sotto voce, flushed
with hope that I, in some small way, might help
defend my future countrymen's beliefs.
"Of course not!" she snaps back. Her eyes betray
no hint of the embarrassed gratitude
I thought I'd be obliged to mitigate.
Yet I persist. "What is it, then?" She stoops
to humor the American *majnoon*.
A slab of what could only be pig flesh
peeks out from underneath the cheese. Her stiff
smile slowly fades. She snatches up my tray
and rushes off. I listen for her voice—
or will it be the captain's?—groveling
in Arabic. The man beside me folds
his newspaper. Its coiled script is all smiles.
The stewardess returns to interrupt
my reverie. She has regained her poise.
"Here is your dinner, sir," she says, straight-faced,
and lays before me what I can't refuse:
a new tray burdened with a crusted lump
of hummus, several withered sticks of carrot,
and a wedge of prehistoric pita bread.
She's gone before I find the wherewithal
to speak. My neighbor sees me hesitate.
He nods expectantly and says, *"Ahlain.*
Welcome." I feel a people's eyes upon me.
I turn aside, ashamed. The window frames
a wide, pale arc of sky, a scalding sun,
and down below an ocean's foreign blue
that speaks as if in tongues, its rumpled water
flowing backward, and white clouds bellying.

Exotic

Amman sprawls, sun-struck, on seven
hills, like a latter-day Rome, only
less so. It was, in fact, once Roman,
as the ruined theater downtown attests,
but today the grown children of sheikhs
drive herds of camel-colored
Mercedes down the steep wadis.
These castoffs of the rich Gulf nations
bellow in the narrow streets of the souk,
where the voices of gold and silver
merchants buzz in their beehive shops.
The cries of muezzins from a dozen mosques
buzz likewise on the outer hills,
blunting their stings against the double-
glazing of the wealthy. A water peddler
hawks the sweat of his brow in a neighborhood
frosted with roses. How wild, how strange
it all seems, as exotic as a rose
thrown in the face of a thirsty man.

Al Badr Street

Each night at eight my neighbor hacks and spits
a lump of sputum from deep in his lungs,
like an old, mad rooster greeting the moon.
All day the air was a blunt instrument
weighted with sunlight, but now colors rise
slowly from hollows, from under the stones,
with the gentleness of roses unfolding
in the warm shadow of a concrete wall.
I step out into the street. The moon floats,
huge, swollen with cold, above the desert.
A stray cat stutters on the filthy lip
of a dumpster. The late light streaks its fur
with rust. A flight of pigeons dips and swirls
as someone whistles from a nearby roof.
Bells shiver at their throats like a ghost of rain.
A shepherd flings a stone, a curse, urging
his flock down the street toward a vacant lot.
Dark wool surrounds me like a cloud of dust.
These moments in another man's routine
are my epiphanies. God seems always
about to speak. My neighbor crows again.
I can imagine, almost, I'm at home.

Houses Made of Hair

1.

It's certain something here is dépaysé,
though whether the concrete apartment blocks
strewn like lagan on the desert floor,
or the *beit shaar* of the Bedouin who camp
in fields between the city's outspread arms,
I could not say. Nor should I call them "fields,"
unless a crop of discarded building stones
mottled with rubbish and greasewood qualifies
as cultivation. I offer up a few
acquired words on either side: *Salaam*
alicum. Keyf ha lak? Children stare. Then one
yells after me, *Hey English!*, and they laugh.
Behind them, tents of brown wool undulate
in the evening air like giant caterpillars
straining to crawl back to the *badiya.*
Or do they writhe like Gullivers against
the guy lines strung by Lilliputian men
who squat nearby? (The similes of empire
catch in my throat like dust. What can I do
but cough them out, or choke?) The women are
invisible. Imagine them inside,
like queen bees, bearing young in their wax cells
or, less than queens now, boiling goat and rice.
Now smell the tart, ripe smoke of burning dung
and hear the desert wind shrill like a bagpipe.
The men's kaffiyehs coil in a clypeal swath
about their heads, their fingers flickering
like tibia and tarsus, counting blessings
on the black coral beads of their *masbahas.*
You could almost say each man is like a bead,
a monad carved from some colonial beast,
for as Miss Doolittle might once have said,

They're all Jack Jones in a bleedin' waste. No wonder
they cling hard to themselves, like drowning men.

2.

Despite the racket and stink of goats grazing
under their bedroom windows, the denizens
of the more convenient, modern world seem fond
of their shiftless neighbors. Often now they dream
of a carnallite and greensand wilderness,
of riding without bridle, bit, or rowel
on a steed whose neck curves like a crescent moon,
whose nose could fit into a china cup.
With daylight, most shake off such fantasies,
though now and then a housewife laughingly
ululates to welcome her husband home.
Then the Bedu boys, tethering their goats
for milking, pause and listen in amazement
to these fine mondaines. A Filipino maid
washes the children's hands as an Egyptian
street sweep leaves his broom. His orange jumpsuit
glows in the early dusk in the Nimri's yard
as he fills a separate trough around each bush.
A muezzin warbles from a nearby mosque.
The faithful lift their heads, hungry for words
such as Gabriel might whisper to sustain them
in the old ignorance of familiar times,
when everything is in its proper season,
and nothing is that is not in its place.

The Ninth Month

"This is the book in which there is no doubt."
The imam's nasal certainty enthralls
the faithful, and I mimic their delight,
touching my forehead to the frayed prayer rug
until the oils and unguents of my brow
shine like an offering on the clotted wool.
He might as well be calling, "Simon says . . ."
and me slow as an insect dipped in honey.
Everything I do or think seems backwards.
I wish I had not stopped here, however much
the mosque sashayed oasis-like on the rough
volcanic plain, its pale-blue, blistered walls
limpid and trembling in the liquid heat,
a concrete mirror of my thirst. But when
the muezzin's muddy call came laboring
from a loudspeaker balanced clumsily above
the door, I longed to hear Muhammad's voice,
swollen with holy words, his syllables
slurred by the fermented honey Gabriel
had poured into his ears. The thought of such food
sent tremors through my belly, which had gone
empty of everything but breath all day.
How does the saying go? In Ramadan,
the fast begins when white thread can be told
from black. So, like a tourist in this house
of hunger, I put by food to savor words.
Or should I say, their sounds? Or the idea
of what escapes me when I hear them spoken?
"Hamdullilah"—Thanks be to God—I know
enough to echo unfamiliar sounds and not
to eat left-handed, hold a holy book
below my belt, or pray with unclean feet.
Stiff-necked, I raise my head. The imam's words
flutter their chitinous wings in my empty gut.

I open my parched mouth and hear, or think
I hear, a kind of song, like the glacial drip
of the *fouwara* in the mosque's courtyard:
a song, indeed, after the dust of sight-
seeing among the caliphs' desert castles
where the wind shrills through narrow windows keen
as locusts humming on the Baptist's tongue.
Here, on the verge of milk and honey, nothing
grows as plentifully as words. Even the goats
and camels speak more often than they feed,
or so I fancy in this long ninth month
of taming my own capricious appetite,
imagining their gossip by the manger,
never doubting their mouths are full of seeds.

A True Story

Damned fool to make a hash of it like that.
Is this what comes from wanting to make art
out of the Middle East's sun-baked back streets?
Or from some larger inability
ever to escape one's foible-ridden self?
God knows I've tried. You judge with what success.

Wherever one begins, it's soon apparent
that the living water he imbibed years since
still seethes like a smothered fountain in his gut.
So what? No harm was done, one might well say.
And how could he have spurned the proffered cup,
though cracked and pitted, bearing traces of
God knows how many lips besides his own,
without an unforgivable hauteur?
He felt like an ambassador of sorts,
albeit penned in tourist class. He thought
he had a nation's honor to uphold.
Or maybe it was something to live down.
Sometimes he sensed his shadow gesturing
behind his back, though whether swaggering
like John Wayne's ample shade toward center stage
or shrinking from the midday desert sun
that spotlit all of his deformities,
he couldn't tell. He tried to shrug it off.
Weekends, he'd brave the natives' knowing looks
and circumnavigate the neighborhood.
At first, he merely smiled and nodded left
and right; then, feeling bolder, *"Marhaba,"*
says he, in a hearty tone. He butchered it,
of course. But still a voice replied: *"Ahlain."*
"Be welcome here." And where was that, you ask?
Let's say, half living room and half front yard.
Though in the New World it would not have passed

for more than weed-strewn dirt on which some soul
had spread an old wool rug between the road
and what his foreign eyes had misconstrued
at first glance as a cinder-block toolshed.
Should I apologize for his mistake?
Dilate my sympathies again? No thanks.
It took this long to separate myself
from him. And as for those romantic sots
who cant of "tranquil recollections"—well,
they only half-remember what went on.
For all their prattling of things sublime,
they far prefer soft-focus memories,
their mental lenses hazy with a scrim
of Vaseline. Just bring them cheek by jowl
with human bestiality and watch
them build an artful firewall of words.

But in my fit of righteous indignation,
I've left you and my faux self dangling.
Imagine, if you will, this scene: two men,
one old, one young—a father and his son?—
reclined sideways along the rug's worn nap,
their elbows propped on sacks of winter wheat,
in such a posture as could well bespeak
the moral high ground of hard work just done.
Picture the swollen evening sun, past ripe,
dripping its syrup in your dazzled eyes.
And this: behind the men, a girl, 19
perhaps, perched on a battered, velvet couch
beside what might in better light have been
her grandmother. The old man flings a word;
the girl jumps up to fetch an old brass tray
on which three glasses faintly steam. The tea
is very sweet; a few bruised mint leaves spin
in rusty eddies.
                    Stop. Before you drink
this all in, empathetic spirit, think
of the cost if you internalize these words:
Like anything, the picturesque is built
of clay and wattles, whose exotic sound

misleads the reader like a realtor's praise
for "rustic plumbing." Can you live with that?
Then picture what it costs if you refuse,
and quickly—hesitation will be read
as sniffing disrespect. The tea grows cold.

He drank. They motioned him to sit. He sat.
They offered him some fractured English words.
He strained to catch a few familiar sounds,
repeating what he heard; his hosts would nod
or shake their heads. He tried some Arabic.
The conversation hobbled back and forth,
strung on their gestures like a puppet show.
He felt an awkward understanding grow.
They farmed a vacant lot across the street
still choked with rubble from the nouveau riche
monstrosities that overshadowed it.
They had no horse or plow, though years ago
they had been rich goldsmiths in Palestine.
And then the Six Day War spun Fortune's wheel
until its axle split.
                    The metaphor
is mine, of course—an effort to bring home
the fat of their loss in a few lean words.
They offered up a richer image though,
ripened in anger past all stomaching:
And did he know Israeli soldiers played
chess with the heads of Arab children? God
forgive his silence. What was there to say?
No, he knew nothing, nothing but the pale
imperial pabulum he'd been fed since birth:
Forgive us our trespasses as we forgive . . .
Their faith seemed absolute. They called on God
to witness, they had heard this tale
from relatives who'd fled to Lebanon,
who'd called on God to witness it was true.

Forgive my lack of silence. They have played
me like a pawn, through him, and even now
I cannot tell if it was their intent

to distance me from who they thought I was,
or if they simply longed for company
in the empty bitterness of their belief.
But what has all of this to do with you?
Perhaps just this: These words inhabit you
now, briefly, animate as your own breath.
Without you, they are nothing, as he is.
My life is fiction, as I've partly learned
through spinning out this tapestry of words,
its fabric draped across the foreign field
of my experience, where you now pause
as I did, years since, on a threadbare rug,
imagining, I hope, beneath each fold
and bump, some real thing, though invisible.
So I imagine you, the mottled light
cupped now like living water in your eyes
as they pace back and forth the way they might
watching an old man fingering the dark
prayer beads on his *masbaha,* each small click
a sound in which I'd have you hear a loss
you cannot feel as other than your own.

Sheikh Majnoon

would never pause to worry as I do
about mixed metaphors. He contradicts
himself on principle. "Words are a curse.
They tempt wise men to think their thinking's thought.
Even a rock knows better." Then, to prove
his point, perhaps, or punctuate his lapse
from silence, he kicks a good-sized stone.
It doesn't budge. His expletives resound
like Dr. Johnson's "Thus!" The sheikh loves stuff
and nonsense. Nothing less. He'd grunt and hop
about like this without a second thought,
but generally it never comes to that.
His motto might be "No ideas, just things,"
among which he would count these words the way
Ben Sikran holds a gold piece on his tongue.
So much for hospitality, one thinks:
His tent no doubt is threadbare and his tea
is thin. He'd dress in rags, like Lear's Poor Tom,
except, like us, he's no one else's fool.
Indeed, his poverty is ours, or ought to be, of mind
and body both. Yes, we should have such luck.
To chatter like rocks through broken teeth,
to hesitate like rain before it falls,
to vibrate like the purple air at dusk,
each needs a barrenness I haven't got.
And yet I ooh and aah, hoping to form
a word that sounds an echo of the sheikh's
palatial palate. Or I cup my hands
as if it might be possible to hold
his emptiness, and molecules of air
dance like a host of angels on my palms.

Shit

There is often a virulent contagion in a confident tone.
—John Tyndall, *Fragments of Science for Unscientific People*

1.

I've held my tongue. Hell, bitten it.
(Who wants to say they've written shit?)
Some things don't "lend themselves" to verse,
but there are others even worse:
the topics everyone avoids,
like feces, phlegm, and hemorrhoids.
Although they are ubiquitous,
you rarely hear these things discussed.
Even sweetened by a dulcet style
human effluvia are vile.
Our tastes lean toward the clean and bland.
Our bodies are like foreign lands
that we're too squeamish to explore.
It seems we're what we most abhor.
What was I thinking, thinking I'm
right to write this, even in rhyme?

2.

For months my mother's admonition
when she took me shopping as a kid
served as my tourist's mantra: "See with
your eyes and not your hands." It wasn't
hard. Despite my longing for local
color and outlandish incident,
the CDC's health warnings had me
imagining my building's rusty
rooftop water tank teeming with E.
coli, salmonella, cholera.
I stayed away from uncooked fruits and
vegetables, eschewed ice cubes, shellfish,
and uncooked meat. I took my water
bottled, boiled, or bubbly, doubling

my local grocer's sales of Saffra.
For months I let fear dictate desire.

3.

But if I was reluctant to embrace
the land, the land felt no reciprocal
reserve, it seems. It played the perfect host,
indulging my peculiarities,
pooh-poohing my inflated fears, and then
extending a microbial tender
of its regard. And what else could I do
but let it make itself at home in me?
It clasped me in an inside-out embrace
and clinched the deal. I clenched my sweaty fists
and squatted, shaking, feverish, above
a hole set in a square of porcelain
that passed in those parts for a toilet bowl.
My soles still feel the indentations of
the ribbed footholds; and now my fingers shrink
from cold, slick tiles like those I clung to then.

4.

Anthropomorphic b.s.? Alright. Why not? If I remake the land in my
own image, am I doing violence to the truth? Adam was named for
red clay, the clay from which, to which, dust to dust, we all come
and go. Potassium and iron, calcium and zinc. Mix a little earth with
water and voilà! I'm not only made in nature's image, I *am* nature's
image. So why not turn my body's mirror back on the land?

Of course there's more to it than that. Consider a living cell: Sim-
ple, as organisms go, it responds to stimuli in predictable ways. So
at what stage do cells acquire a consciousness of themselves? When
gathered into a tissue? Organized into an organ? Compiled into a
vertebrate? I'd say it happens when language intervenes between
the stimulus and the response. Then language holds a mirror up to
nature and flesh becomes word. Because language is metaphorical,
the self can be seen as separate from the seeing. Language provides
a space outside the self in which the self performs. It is the source
of our cells' collective ability to consider themselves. Like this:

5.

My belly's calm tonight.
I wouldn't ruminate like this, of course,
if it were not. And it's not
as if it often isn't, though it does
still trouble me sometimes
with vague, confused alarms
that I interpret as the aftershocks
of that abdominal upheaval
when ignorant armies of bacteria
laid my body waste. Nine days and nights
I heaved myself from bed and shat
and staggered back to bed again, until
my misery had clogged the building's antique pipes.
Thank God the neighbors raised a stink.
My landlord traced the problem to its source,
and so my own extremity relieved itself.

6.

If making light of what I suffered seems
in questionable taste, it proves at least
that words have weight. In my experience
they burrow through the mind the way those germs
entrenched themselves in my intestines.
Once certain words make certain neurons fire,
their grumblings echo in my memory
for years. Somehow they physically inscribe
themselves in me; my mental chemistry
is different once they've wormed their way, by grace
or guile, into my consciousness. My self.
A poem may look bland and innocent
as bottled water or a fresh-peeled fig,
but once you've sampled it the words may prove
more virulent than any previous
idea you'd entertained. How do you feel?

7.

Zuhair was my savior. A selfless man, he
ran a private medical laboratory
and admitted it, though I would have tried to
       run if, like him, I'd

gone to an apartment to check the plumbing
only to be met at the front door by a
desiccated zombie. But Zuhair went down-
       stairs and brought back a

jar that, filled, he took with him to his office.
Something called "Flagyll" would soon fix what ailed me,
he declared, with confidence born of hands-on
       knowledge. But Flagyll,

while it fought my malady, hit me almost
harder with fresh nausea, chills, and headaches.
Still, it worked. So praise Zuhair: wise man, brother,
       loveliest landlord.

8.

After my recovery, I dream heaven harbors no euphemisms.
No "powdering of noses," no "bathrooms," no figures of speech
of any kind. No "afterwards." Only fountains of cloud
in which the chosen practice what they preach:
"Cleanliness is next to godliness." "Waste not, want not."
Manna melts in their mouths and bathes their veins
in such liquor they have no cause to crap.
No flatulence. No sweat. The godly are divinely clean
without the need for soap, shampoo, or frankincense.
They strut and preen, naked as babies, without shame,
though these days no one notices, not since their flesh
turned back into the Word from which it came.
They can't recall the odor of their own armpits.
No pain or illness touches them. They are immune
to sadness. They have no choice but lift their voices
to rejoice. They can't remember any other tune.

9.

"After great pain a formal feeling comes."
A need for order, for words to stiffen
our hearts and minds around an axiom.
But my form is loose as a camel's when
it bends its knees outwards at journey's end.
My nerves aren't ceremonious. Just numb.
Or slovenly. Having blown where the wind
wished, they have gone slack in the sudden calm.

We each have an idea of home—
what becomes us—what we become.

What am I getting at? I'm not myself.
The desert wind whistles through me. Nomads
roam my body's wasteland. I follow
as best I can, lost in this Persian Gulf
of the mind, this poem, my heart's Baghdad.
The land's alive in me. I can't let go.

II. Impostors

Impostors

And surely you recall, if I see you as you are,
how I, myself, played the good ape of nature.
—L'Ombra di Capocchio

With what glee Dante might have once pronounced
me damned, my moral dishabille laid bare
as Bocca's skull when, in his sweet and nuanced

style, the poet yanked out fistfuls of his hair.
But in which ditch would his deliberate
bon mots have me penned? Where Mohamet's scarred

carcass, like some haruspical exhibit,
walks with his bowels and severed member dangling
from a split trunk? Or sunk waist-deep in shit

among the flatterers? Perhaps my "sin,"
if that's the word I want, will break new ground
in Dante's underworld, requiring

the Mantuan to sing another round.
—But who'm I kidding? Walt's barbaric yawp
had been there, done that, years before I found

myself in Jordan, on a whistle-stop
tour of that foreign land. What hope have I
of conjuring extravagance to top

his multitudes? I'm not that sort of guy.
But then, who is? Of course, some people fool
themselves; but there's no need to magnify

my story: Even its most minuscule
events loom large. This smacks of pride? Well, call
it that, but still I think, like Dante, you'll

be better off (in metaphorical
if not financial terms) for having heard
my story. So I start the canticle:

How many months in Jordan had I frittered
away when Ghazi asked me to his home
in Madaba? At first, I'd felt awkward

and rarely strayed far from my humdrum Umm
Udhayna neighborhood, with its Pizza Hut
and supermarket, liquor stores and Tom

and Jerry's. Now I'd do the opposite,
though it's too late. Thank God at last a soldier
in the Royal Guard dragged me from my closet—

although my Arabic was so unsure
it still strikes me as near miraculous
his invitation pierced the armature

of my dumb stare. But, like Odysseus,
I finally fared forth, with Ghazi's scrawled
directions for a guide. I should have guessed

I'd face a trial or two. For one, he'd called
up all his neighbors. And the living room
of his small, cinderblock abode was dolled

up like some Third World opera. For whom?
As if I couldn't guess. *"Saba al khair,"*
I muttered, shaking hands beneath an heirloom

hawk's glass-eyed gaze. It perched with its threadbare
wings spread as if to shield the old TV
that served it as a pedestal. "From where

this?" I ventured, in my broken *Arabee.*
A flock of hands took sudden flight, their gyres
retracing (and a bit more graphically

than narrative economy required)
how Ghazi's father, as a young man, caught
the bird, bare-handed. It had just expired

in gory pantomime when Ghazi brought
the coffee out and mercifully cut short
the taxidermic denouement. I'd thought

26

to loll about on Ghazi's davenport
and spend a couple hours making nice
like an ambassador-at-large of sorts,

sample quaint customs, and then scram. No dice.
I'd barely started feeding my own hunger
for the Orphic, when I couldn't help but notice

they'd pegged *me* as a cabinet of wonders,
and everybody wanted in. ‏هل فهمت؟‏
A thousand and one questions—or maybe slanders

for all I knew, since now and then I glimpsed
a knot of neighbors point at me and laugh.
I smiled at everyone. The small room brimmed

with awkward pauses. At last, on my behalf
I reckoned, Ghazi gestured toward the door.
I followed, grateful as a fatted calf.

Too late, I saw that he had something more
in mind: Two neighbors lay in wait outside.
One held a sheikh's robe like a semaphore.

I didn't like the way the other eyed
my Oxford shirt. I feigned a puzzled look,
but they were having none of it. One pried

my shirt off while the other man unhooked
my belt and stripped me to my underpants.
I wilted like a schmuck (well, let's say *schnook*)

who's duped into more confident men's hands.
Then Ghazi dressed me in a *thawb:* a long,
white sheath that covered up my deodands,

at least. A black robe, trimmed with gold along
its seams, was next, and then a red-and-white
kaffiyeh, held on by a braided thong.

I looked a fool, which is to say I might
have been mistaken by a passerby
as thinking clothes could make the man. They fit

well, though, and as there were no passersby,
I flirted with the soothing thought they meant
the whole thing as a private honor. So I

was mortified when Ghazi, too hell-bent
on some wild scheme to notice my cold feet,
walked over to the car I'd had to rent

and motioned me into the driver's seat.
His henchmen piled into the back; their doors
slammed shut on any hope they'd be discreet

about how easy it had been to lure
me into impropriety. "You drive,
Mr. John!" they cried. I drove. I'm still not sure

which kind god saw me through that day alive
(the one that watches over women in
tight skirts, I'd guess: The *thawb* wrapped like a sleeve

around my legs). I'm sure we came within
an inch of death, because the damned kaffiyeh
billowed about my head like a huge foreskin.

At least I'll die in style, I thought—though, Allah
knows, a sheikh's garb's not the style I'd choose.
But we made it to the heart of Madaba

where Ghazi stopped us, dashed up to a news
kiosk, and came back brandishing a rented
camera. "What's Arabic for 'cheese'?" I mused,

growing increasingly disoriented
as Ghazi's eager cries of *"Duri!" "Schmall!"*
"Yameen!" led us through the garbage-scented

streets to a quaint old church. Somehow, the smell
that wafted from the overflowing dumpsters
lent the town a piquant flavor—a small,

backwards reminder of a gift of myrrh
and frankincense, perhaps—that made me feel
I'd reached the Holy Land at last. A tour

bus parked nearby confirmed it. No time to steel
myself before a large, myopic, red-
haired matron from Louisiana reeled

me in—a desert angler's prize—and said
to her bemused husband, "Oh dahlin', look!"
He did. "Now take my picture with this Bed-

oo-whine!" Her tone suggested she would brook
no argument, not even from so pale
a specimen of Arabness. She'd hooked

me good. So I tried to hide behind the veil
through which she saw me, fearing that she'd find
me out and blame her blunder on some guile

of mine. *"Salaam alicum. Key'fik?"* I mimed
something I hoped resembled dignified
assent: *"Ma'andeesh mehni"*—I don't mind—

not thinking of myself as having lied,
since Mrs. Bluster never understood
a word. (And yet, her failure qualified

as my success, as if I'd tried to hood-
wink her.) After this tourist photo op,
I slunk back to my waiting friends, who would,

I thought, be gloating over what a dope
they'd made of me; but no one even smirked.
In fact, they looked like tourists, too, who hoped

to find some sights worth seeing in that kirk
besides myself. I joined them in the aisle,
forgetting my present form beside the work

of Byzantine mosaicists: Their tiles
of ocher, teal, cerulean, mimicked
the land I stood on, stone by stone, compiled

into a map of "Palestine" (*sic*
in guidebooks printed in the Arab world).
There were Jerusalem, Hebron, Kerak,

and the Dead Sea. A boat with its sails furled
like an empty serpent skin was rowed by two
disfigured passengers along the curled

backs of the sea's stone swells. I wondered who
had turned these pale-skinned images of men
into a pair of speckled eggs that grew

hands, legs, a foot. And did their passive sin—
doubled by being born as likenesses
of God's anthropic handiwork and then

reswaddled in such obvious disguises—
make blasphemous their presence in God's home,
as Deuteronomy advises us,

because they had been wounded in the stones?
There was a thought I'd rather not explore:
Such speculations cut too near the bone.

I found the others and we moved outdoors.
I thought that we'd head home, but I was wrong.
Ghazi, it seemed, had planned a full-length tour

of Jordan, sparing neither Sturm nor Drang.
I don't exaggerate. At least, not much.
My mind is its own place, and if I longed

like a drunk dreaming of a fifth of scotch
to lose myself in its familiar wastes,
I'm not the only one who lives life kvetch-

as-kvetch-can. Aren't we all a bit two-faced?
I am. I made the Holy Land a hell
of devils mocking me, then gained a taste

for self-demotion and began to tell
myself that I deserved their mockery.
O vain white man! O Western Belial!

And ain't it odd that such buffoonery
should give me back a sense of the control
I'd lost when Ghazi took my dungarees?

Yet when he had me stop outside a hole-
in-the-wall falafel shop, I paid with good
grace for enough kebobs to feed the whole

damn crew and slowly felt my martyr's mood
begin to lift. We climbed back in the car.
I drove us out of town while Ghazi chewed

the fat with his rear guard. We'd not gone far
when he decided it was time for lunch.
I eased us slowly off the road's hot tar

and parked. We found some shade beneath a bunch
of scraggly olive trees and ate the lamb
with bread and spicy onions rolled and pinched

between the first two fingers and the thumb
of our right hands. The authenticity
of every morsel filled me with aplomb,

hardly hampered by the infelicity
of paper plates. Still chewing his last bite,
Ghazi tossed his plate aside—a nicety

I tried to imitate, but couldn't quite.
Despite their protests and attempts to hold
me back, I couldn't but be impolite

and gather all their trash with mine—the soiled
napkins and bits of greasy bread—and stuff
it quickly in the trunk. Then I cajoled

a few indulgent smiles from Ghazi's gruff
display of injured pride—as if I'd tried
to clean his living room—and soon enough

our car was toiling up Mount Nebo's side
like Moses' ass-drawn cart. Two old school buses
followed and dropped off hordes of flashing-eyed

schoolgirls from Salt. A couple of the hussies
laughed at my frock and cried, "Hey, English!" like
they'd caught me hiding in the bulrushes

trying to be a Lawrence look-alike.
But, undismayed, I waved at them and smiled
in a way I trusted was at least lifelike,

if not quite doing justice to my style
of dress. They seemed astonished by my chutzpah,
although they stood beside a garish steel

shed (built to house the old basilica)
that showed a comparable sangfroid. Even
more gaudy was the huge, coiled replica

of Moses' bronze serpent, mirroring the Son
of Man, His arms spread on the Cross, which marks
the prophet's first and only glimpse of Canaan.

He may have died of disappointment: Stark,
tan cliffs drop to a moiled, beige haze of hills
that undulate across a plain pockmarked

by countless stone-filled wadis' yearly spill
of dirt and rubble. One would have to bring
little to this harsh land but the willful

habits of faith to find it promising.
The air was like L.A.'s (on a bad day)
or the dun smoke I pictured issuing

in spent coils from the nondescript gateway
of Hell. Then Ghazi pointed. "Jerusalem."
A silence. It was all he had to say.

It would have been the *terminus ad quem*
of the day's trials to see that holy place.
But life is hardly ever like a poem,

until we dress our dingy, commonplace
experience in the exotic rags
of metaphor. Truly, in medias res,

I couldn't see a thing. Thick dust swagged
above the lowlands, its hungry festoons
swallowing the city whole. When Ghazi dragged

me back to the car, the Byzantine ruins
squatted there still, in such plain view it seemed
vain to have looked for anything but tombs

and ashes in this desert god's demesne.
Oddly, now, no one noticed what I wore.
No catcalls, laughs, or jibes broke the serene

ennui that settled over me like one more
black sheikh's robe, woven, it seemed, without respect
for such surroundings. Soon the engine snored

under the hood and Ghazi's friends were sacked
out in the back. The sun stared blankly down.
But no, not disrespect: more like a lack

of any source of shade—outside one's own
body, of course. The parched earth makes one's flesh
feel like a damp oasis, overgrown

with strange fruits, weeds, and orchids, rank and lush
and alien. Only a proper scorn
for self reclaims the self from such riches;

a goat-hair shirt, forty days fasting, thorns
pushed through the plump ball of the thumb: These signs
of disrespect were each in their way born

of love—the same love, possibly, behind
Ghazi's investment of my foreignness
in local trappings. Was it asinine

of me to entertain such thoughts? Yes,
given that I was steering us through hairpin
curves down a mountain road with something less

than total concentration. Ghazi's chin
dropped several feet as one wide turn gave him
a less obstructed view down to Ma'in

than he'd thought possible. Strains of a hymn,
in strangled chorus, rose from the back seat,
where Ghazi's friends, bolt upright, looking grim,

no longer ambled in the fields of sleep.
Only I was calm, behind my billowing
headdress, gaily declining their repeated

offers to take the wheel. (My easygoing
attitude was absent driving home
when, *sans chapeau,* I saw the harrowing

descent myself.) Sharp-edged and honeycombed,
high cliffs encircled us, like some huge hive
of red clay, long abandoned. Our eardrums

popped, and we swallowed hard. As small weeds thrive
in the crevices of boulders, so I felt
only by being small could I survive

in that immense bowl, hollowed out like Hell
from the reluctant earth. I stopped beside
a stone tollhouse, marked "Thermal Springs," to shell

out more dinars: A bored attendant eyed
my clothes and looked decidedly nonplussed.
But after just a few words from my guide,

he grinned, saluted me, and let us pass.
The parking lot was for a pseudo-swank
hotel where tourists paid to have a fuss

made over their infirmities: They sank
like souls in limbo into steaming mud-
baths, or they floated in huge porcelain tanks

of water spiked with Dead Sea salt. I should
refrain from sarcasm, of course—or mock
myself, if anyone—for even Herod

could hardly have out-Heroded the shock
I felt when Ghazi and his trusty lads,
without a word, stripped off their shoes and socks,

then shirts and pants, and stood before me clad
in matching bathing trunks. "Son of a bitch,"
I muttered helplessly as Ghazi led

the way along the left bank of a ditch
from which a yellow, faintly sulfurous
steam clambered. Where rocks pocked the stream, a rich

gurry of algae, like a greenish pus,
coated the water. Piles of excrement
ripened in shadows where lost souls before us

had squatted, offering their compliments,
perhaps, to some foul god who'd claimed that gorge.
The heat grew more intense as our descent

brought us below a waterfall that surged
down the opposing cliff in scalding rills,
as though an ancient and infernal forge

had overheated, cracked its base, and spilled
thick braids of liquid metal down the rock.
So it was almost of my own free will

that I allowed myself to be defrocked
again and did my best to act urbane
in just my jockey shorts. The culture shock

was fierce. But once we hit the stream, the pain
of being boiled alive like lobsters proved
distracting. Simply trying to maintain

my balance was a trick when slick rocks moved
beneath my pale, bare feet. I nearly quit
when I could see they meant to climb above

the falls. I didn't think I had the grit
to play at Sisyphus, hauling the stone
of my own body up that slope. And yet

I'd come that far. Something (testosterone?)
made me go on, although on hands and knees,
trying to save my thinly-clad tailbone.

At last, I looked up, panting, and could see
Ghazi perched above me on a ledge.
And so I inched my way up by degrees

until I reached the backdrop my alleged
comrades had chosen for the day's climax,
which simply was to sit in our abridged

attire with the sun's full weight against our backs
as brackish, scalding water splashed and played
across our legs. I tried to look relaxed.

Oddly, I *was* relaxed. This blunt cascade
drowned out the talking that we couldn't do
and laid to rest all need to play charades.

O differences, dissolve! Suspicions, shoo!
Awash in agape, I rhapsodized.
And so I made my Whitmanesque debut,

with armpits bared, until a new surmise
troubled my mind (although it seemed absurd)
that what I felt was just a new disguise.

Fuck it, I thought, I've had enough of words.
I closed my eyes. Then Ghazi took my hand,
and for a moment, neither of us stirred.

Only the raw sunburn that dyed my bland
skin red as native desert rock announced
my stubborn strangeness in that foreign land.

—⌒ఌ

Wouldn't that make a model ending, if
I left us hand in hand, informal, sunk
in a pool of fellow feeling, as the stiff

crease-lines of closure draped our parboiled trunks
like flattering new suits? And did I earn
the exit of my choice? Kidnapped by lunk-

heads, dragged through half the Middle East, sunburned,
paraded like a freak in sideshow togs,
then next to none. . . . What little I have learned

will haunt the margins of this monologue;
as for the rest, I hear some critics raise
their voices to object: "This waterlogged

pundit does not know jack, and all he says
is condescending, boastful, or dead wrong."
I dodge by self-inflicting their touchés—

knowing at least a few notes in this song
will hit their mark. Of course that mark is me,
or so I hope, refined by fire along

these better lines: no more the far-flung country
bumpkin or post-imperial naïf
in metaphorical Bermuda shorts. When Ghazi

reached for my hand, his touch obliged belief.
I'd felt the eastern sun convert my skin
already. So I leaned back in my briefs,

at peace, and stared down idly at the bracken
that grew along the stream, so dense and close
it cast the rocky bank in shadow. Then

the branches quivered, shook—a great hooked nose
appeared, and Dante followed. His frown expressed
disgust at how I dallied, as Virgil froze

his tongue when Dante chattered on, obsessed
with the torments some poor sinner wallowed in.
I'd not lie if I said I couldn't rest

under his glassy stare. It seemed my sin
was coming home to roost. I'd almost swear
he spoke then, in the voice of a Bedouin:

"Get up now. Even in your underwear,
you're still a tourist in this life; your art,
like mine, rests in not resting anywhere.

"Go on, and don't be tempted by the heart's
fleabag hotels, oases of a finite
love for this world." I'd have told the old fart

to shove it, but I knew that he was right.
The world lay all around me, an abundance
so palpable that only God could ghostwrite

such interwoven joy and pestilence.
Each grain of sand clamored in broken English,
calling its name, until I longed for silence,

knowing that one day I would get my wish.

III. The Invisible World

The Invisible World

One morning, when I fancied all the world,
from dewy sward to thorny spray, lay furled
before me, needing only proper words
said reverently to bare its pithy innards,
I walked into the desert, looking for
the choicest of great Nature's metaphors.

The cupboard was bare.
Each rock bobbed passively on the literal
swell of sunlight; each pebble and
every grain of sand
being
      none-other-than
                itself.
I'd never known such clarity,
such barrenness. Words
were next to useless.
Even the bare word "rock" appeared,
not so much in- as hyper-adequate:
It posited a class and thereby failed
the individual. In desperation, as it were,
I touched on "stone," then "scree" and "gravel,"
even the farfetched "gabbro," "tuff," "alluvium."
I babbled. "Isomorphic microcline
of sodium aluminum silicate?"
I cast about me for a spell
but couldn't mirror back a single metamorphic lump,
much less the whole damn landscape.
The world might just as well have been invisible
as any ghoul or djinni
for all that I could make of it. My iambs
stumbled over piles of rubble insubstantial
as these words.

And well you might then say: *The sun clung briefly*
to the humped horizon by a single dirty
fingernail. A bone-dry darkness guttled the hills.
I followed that road as far as I could, for miles
it seemed, to a nondescript gateway. When the haze cleared,
I looked no further. Bitumen. Asphalt. The night came down
like tar. Behind me, the footsteps of someone long dead
still echoed their primitive podics: Macadam, I'm Adam.
Then something else. Dammit, I'm mad! I thought.
It was the Tin Man's heart again, somewhere ahead:
a thin, frail drone like a cardiac monitor,
a voice you might have grown to love.

Now that we've heard each other's words, spoken
as if with our own lips, in the mind's ear,
I stoop again in memory to touch
the blank page of the ground. A rich ink stirs
in my veins. Can you feel the rocks' rough crust,
or smell their vivid longing to be dust?
I call it your desire (you call it mine)
to be a fragment and a multitude.
For dust will drink the corkscrew script of blood
scrawled all about the sacrificial beast
and dream of rendering life's code again.
But blood in dust is disappearing ink.
I long for something solid in my hands,
a rock, a small epiphany of earth,
firmer than the flesh to which I'm wed.
My palms and fingers form a shallow cup
in which an inch-long feldspar chunk reclines
with greater gravity than water would.
I trust that you can feel its weight, my friend,
and, as you value your good name, you will
indulge me in this one apostrophe—
it stands for everything that I have left
out of necessity (why would I lie?):

"O Peter's pinky! Prophet's phalanx shaft!
O bone-chip risen through its mother's flesh!
The scattered details of this land cohere

in infinite recursion, stone by stone,
unto the last electron, and beyond.
Yet how to name them? How convey the fact
much less the substance of their mattering?
Sometimes language is a rich oasis,
sometimes a desert, where my mind repairs
and, willy-nilly, speaks itself in fits
and starts. I watch the random glyphs and sounds
fall into place as if of my free will
and grammar's sweet, pervasive eloquence,
in much the way (I trust) that quarks and leptons,
atoms, gravel, hills—our minds themselves—
have coalesced out of the tendency
of things. But am I merely tendency?
Or can I translate thought to action, find
originality in pattern, read in brute
experience some semblance of a self?
Dear stone, become Rosetta for me now!
Awake and answer me, insensate clod!"

And latent in my hands, the rock replies:

The Empty Quarter

In early spring, here in the Rub 'al Khali,
Gabriel swings his goad over the humped backs
of swollen clouds. They roar like angry camels
and thunder toward the fields of the fellahin.
At night, I dream of grass so green it speaks.
But at noon, even the dry chatter of djinn
leaves the wadis. The sun lowers its bucket,
though my body is the only well for miles.
A dropped stone calls back from the bottom
with the voice of a starving locust: Make it
your wish, *habibi,* and the rain will walk
over the dry hills of your eyes on tiptoes
as the poppies weave themselves into a robe
to mantle the broad shoulders of the desert.
The words uncoil like smoke from a smothered fire,
rising leisurely out of me as though to mark
where a castaway has come aground at last.
And yet I have not spoken. My voice limps
on old bones, its legs too dry and brittle
to leap like a barking locust into song.
But I imagine what was said or might
be said by some collective throat about
the plowman loving best the raw, turned earth,
or the caliph longing for his desert lodge,
where *ghoulem* whisper like the wind at prayer,
and poppies bow their gaudy heads toward Mecca,
each one mumbling a different word for dust.

The Hospitality of Sheikh Majnoon

He is as in a field a silken tent. . . .

Oh, but it is . . . dirty? Sure. But vain words such as these,
rising like goldfish gasping after flakes of dried bread,
are the pets of a privilege that's foreign to the sheikh.
His poverty should need no introduction. He is famous
for his table's barrenness, for sending guests home hungry,
for the slender majesty of his thinking. Absentminded?
Well, if he's not all there, at least he never hesitates
to let a stranger tag along. But does this, in itself,
deserve our thanks? Do thoughts turned heavenward excuse a lack
of mutton fat and too few almonds in the sheikh's *mensaf*?
It would be nice to say "no doubt"—except denial
of the flesh so clearly smacks of bourgeois propaganda,
these days no one but a fool buys into poverty
as virtue. That's our sheikh! His tent throbs in the midday sun,
the woven goat hair stiff with wind-blown sand. A clay jar, gray
and bare as a desert hill, holds a scant handful of green,
unroasted coffee beans. He puts one underneath his tongue
and tips the rest into an antique mortar's scarred brass bowl.
He lights a few thin sticks of greasewood; as the pale flames
fumble into life, he slowly grinds the beans to dust.
He pours three fingersworth of water from a nearby seep
into a pot caked white with calcium, then adds the grounds
and then the bean he sheltered in his mouth. At last he sits
on his heels to wait. He doesn't speak. His skin is crisp and tan
as cardamom. The coffee, when it's done, is thin, but hot.
And that is all. The sheikh's sparse hospitality does not
pile cushions on the rocky ground, or fan away the nagging
flies of hunger. Instead, his generosity of spirit
leaves us host to all our own sensations, raw and cooked,
as though our bodies could be tents of silken goat's hair
pitched in the lean fields of Samaria. He loves us all.

The Snow Men

They must not mind the winter
in Amman, the vertical sun
leaning southward, weeks of gray

sky piled above the hills, and rain;
only rarely does the desert wear
a mask of ice dust like a rhyme,

or so I've heard, but when it snows, against
the country's common barrenness
it seems the exhalation of a god,

and all around the town, snow men
rise like ghosts of a New England
winter, as if the land were mirroring

my cool regard, inviting me
to raise this effigy, to bind
an old kaffiyeh to its brow.

The Seventh Circle

In Umm Udhayna, roses lean like drunkards
on the soft shoulders of the evening air.
Their flushed lips mouth
the desert sun's ebullient babble.
Were I to speak, I fear my voice
would pool on the dry surface of things.
The caked earth swallows nothing.
All day revelation drifts
like flakes of fire from the cloudless sky,
until the very bushes in my garden
blaze with eidetic exclamations,
and the burning dust hums
with the muffled voice of God.
When the earth turns its back
on the sun again, as fickle and predictable
as you or I, the solitary rocks unfold
collars of shadow in the sudden chill.
They hunch like con men jealously
guarding the artifice of their rigged shell-games.
I would wager the silt and ashes of my flesh
for one glimpse of the withered pea
called faith. "Here it is," the dust cries,
and, yes, there it is, indeed, one moment, perched
like a pearl on a bivalve tongue,
or like a plastic Christ lapped in the crèche's
tinderbox of straw. I cup both hands
to my ears, wishing to drown out all sound
but this: the ocean murmuring its distant
heave and sigh, and in that slow, heavy seiche,
the camels, white as butter, and the goats
as they begin to speak.

The House of God

In Deir Allah, a ring-straked goat lay dead
among thick tufts of tall blue phlox. Its throat
gaped like a gate to heaven carelessly
thrown wide. Damp blooms tumbled from the wound
like blood-spattered angels stumbling up the rungs
of an inverted ladder. "Holy shit!"
I muttered under my breath (once I'd caught it).
And all I'd wanted was a likely spot
to pee.
      Alright. I wanted more than that.
I'd driven up the Jordan Valley road
to look for Jacob's oil-soaked pillow stone,
the pillar he'd erected like a . . . well,
a finger pointing out the path to God.
My road map led me to a smallish town
just north of As Subayhi: two long rows
of stone and cinderblock that paralleled
Route 65; a service station run,
it seemed, from someone's living room; a store
or two; a "Hair Saloon"; and, just beyond,
this "dreadful" place where, mesmerized, I stood
staring down the gullet of an empty well.

An iridescent halo of green flies
erupted from the carcass, breaking the spell.
Behind me, someone cursed: "Ar-hurm har-häch!"
And who could blame whoever'd overheard
my sotto voce blasphemy? Chalk up
another round to the ugly tourist: I
might just as well have pissed on his wheat fields.
I turned then, timidly, and saw a man,
hunched over, hands on knees, cough, "Har, har, HÄCH!"
and hock a fat, wet looey in the phlox.
He paused a moment, straightened up, and smiled.

"Excuse an old man his infirmities.
But you are young—no matter though I looked
for you these two hours past. I mind the heat
much less than you might think!" His English was
a match for mine—his voice more muscular.
Its rough lines looped around me like a noose:
"Please kneel," he said. I knelt. "Give me the knife."
How did he know I'd stopped that afternoon
to browse a tourist trap outside of Salt
and bought an antique knife, its curved blade etched
with coiled script gathered like an eagle poised
to fall upon its prey? Reluctantly
I handed it to him. It looked as though
I'd end up like the goat—a sacrifice
to some unspecified god's whim. But then,
as if in answer to my fear, he said:
"This beast's soul drains like water from a sponge.
Here, feel the body stiffen with departure."
He pressed my hand against the matted flank.
"Now lay your hand across its eyes and fold
the left ear back. Silence! Be still. You'll feel
a question fill your lungs. Then quickly breathe
into the ear—now, while it offers passage."
Somehow I didn't pause to wonder why
I should perform such patent foolishness.
His phlegm-filled voice was ringing in my ears.
I pinched the goat's ear back against its horn
and leaned in close to offer my mute prayer.
The old man wedged his knife into the curve
below the goat's breastbone and with the sound
of damp cloth ripping split the belly down
to where its penis sprouted like a weed.
And then: A miracle? A hoax? I heard
the words so clearly, yet I couldn't say
whether the old man spoke with the splayed hiss
of a split intestine spewing its pent winds
or if the valved gut itself became a mouth:

> *Your body is a salt sea ringed with weeds,*
> *your soul an eddy of sweet water, slave*

to your body's tides. Yours is a hermit's heart,
though a multitude within you struggles, hand
to foot, to feed the lust that loves a bowl
of porridge better than the Word of God.

Doubt is the angel of our time; and who
among us cares to wrestle with that voice
of burning fennel, or the corduroy
rustle of its crippled wings? And what should we
believe? Our senses? There in the House of God,
I looked around and found myself alone
and upright, with no memory of standing.
At my feet, two lines of flies were glistening
like broken sutures on the beast's split throat.
Its belly was intact. So what is true?
If we could look more closely, would we see
the caprine carcass as it is: its skin
a scud- and cloud-wracked outer atmosphere,
its flesh a play of probability?
The Word of God glows in each atom's heart—
a nest of particles, snarled syllables,
amassed into the grammar of this world.
No wonder we rely on metaphors.
Our deepest certainties are founded on
the rush of sodium along a nerve.
Why doubt the goat could speak? You heard yourself
the dead words whispered in your inner ear.

Third Person

When Hamid opened his eyes, he beheld Nakr and Nkeer, and he spoke to them, asking, "Am I truly dead?" To which the angels answered, "And do you wish either our 'Yea' or 'Nay'?"
—from a Bedouin folktale

As early spring
           grass mumbles
                      in the mouths of sheep
and the chirm of linnets
           reckless with returning
                      haunts the eaves
departure haunts
           the nomad's mind
                      and he imagines
Nakr and Nkeer
           their wings folded
                      in straightjackets
dropping like stones
           on hennaed heels
                      into the slack-
jawed earth
           tongues swollen
                      with questions
are you now
           or have you
                      ever been?
as Nakr ticks
           a jackal's fingerbone
                      against his teeth
and Nkeer sniffs
           behind a handkerchief
                      scented with the zest
of strange fruit
           an odor that clogs
                      the nomad's memory
till even in his
           own imagining
                      he's nothing
other than
           a few words
                      in third person

IV. In Situ

In Situ

A clerk stamps my passport: home. A conveyor belt rattles.
Familiar hands wave behind smudged Plexiglas barricades.

The summer air sprawls like a glutted sphinx, incurious.
Heavy paws damp my shoulders. Crickets purr deep in its throat.

A church bell-tower pins this quaint New England town to earth
like a splayed insect, transcendence wrung from its clenched flesh.

Thick with grease, smoke drifts like a sermon from the pulpit of
the Mathers' charcoal grill. Today's text is the fatted calf.

The fat of the earth clogs all eloquence. It wants a style
as clear and reticent as dust. The granite tang of dirt.

A scrub of weeds and dead leaves covers the earth like locusts.
Above the hills, the sun purses its lips before it sets.

My heart shrinks from the raw, vegetable glut. I am a ghost
of myself, a wisp, invisible as a desert wind.

There is a time for everything, a place. Not here. Not now.
The stone walls that fence these woods inscribe my native milieu.

Sheikh Majnoon in Mufti

After more than twenty hours' travel,
the sheikh, perhaps, may be excused a little
muddleheadedness. Still, he is himself surprised
at his surprise when, notwithstanding all that he has heard,
he staggers up the gangway into Logan's air-conditioned limbo,
parts ways with the common flock, and, at a window
overlooking the broken roofs of Boston tenements, finds
he is the only angel anywhere in sight (Mohammedan
or otherwise). He spends days wandering a labyrinth
of one-way streets, turned back repeatedly by unbridged
waterways, industrial "parks," rivers of concrete. He is lost
and found and lost again. He learns to use quotation marks
ironically and takes to haunting bare commons.
But even there he wonders what Cotton Mather meant
when he described the New World as a "desart."
By then he has a hardened sense of this place as the opposite
of what he'd mean by such a word—were he to use such words.
The midsummer air is thick and resentful;
the horizon rings him in with things. His own flesh thickens
on his wrists and ankles, puffed up like a sponge.
His spirit liquefies. He finds the thought of witchcraft,
in a place like this, absurd. It must have been a metaphor,
he thinks, a sign of how the senses can bewitch the soul.
Soon, indeed, he catches himself glancing over his shoulder,
searching for the eyes he senses staring out of walls,
although he feels invisible in jeans and polo shirt.
Images of home torment him with their unbearable faintness—
ghosts of olive trees, the shadow of a muezzin's voice—
until one night he dreams that he has been condemned
to linger among the ripened grasses of Elysium, surrounded by souls
longing only for the palpable facts of themselves,
unfit for heaven's airy, arid ways.

Humid

Midsummer, and
          it ain't the heat
he says. Who'd disagree? The air
is ripe with possibility.
Dog breath. Stale beer. His own sour flesh.
He rubs his brow on a damp sleeve
then heaves a plastic tub over
the tailgate. Dab and amberjack,
sea robin, grunt. His belly falls
over his belt like a slow surge
of summer light.
          Midafternoon.

Where is our native genius in
all this? Where is Lawrence's "clean"
desert? And where the clarity
of a landscape made of single
grains of sand? The rhythms and the
rhymes of excess haunt the larder
of American poetics.

Later, propped on his own back stoop,
he shucks fish viscera on spread
pages of the *Boston Herald*.
They rustle like a field of corn
on whose horizon a picture
snapped in the Holy Land last night
catches his eye: a city bus
blown inside out, still smoldering.
A few survivors turn their blank
eyes to the camera. No one
speaks. Only the disembodied
narrator drones on about the
victims and their families and

a stranger in a tweed coat stitched
with pipe-bombs and arid motives.

At this distance, what is there to say?
How can he feel, high in the nose,
the acrid loss, the blasphemous
reek of burnt flesh? His own flesh melts
in the day's swelter and lapses
back into life. The thick air rolls
a salty word on its tongue, then
slowly, smacking its lips, swallows.

A Fast of God's Choosing

Past one and still no vendor's cart in sight,
no minimarts here on the Freedom Trail.
My hollow belly moans a kind of song,
like the west wind whistling hosannas
under the vault of the Old South Meeting House:

"When hunger sucks the marrow from your bones,
whittle an octave's worth of fingering
along your fibula and then your soul
will pipe a song to make you weep for God.
And though tears linger on the desert of your lips,
resist their salty frankness, for it masks
a deeper thirst than you should care to know.
No, do not speak. Words smack of damnable
conceit. Which of us knows God's ways? Your lips
should crack with thirst before you fold your breath
in speech. Thank God when he humiliates
your flesh beyond the compass of mere words.
A plump blackberry like a ripe bon mot
could spell damnation if it made you think
the fullness of a summer afternoon
meant jack. The scent of summer honeysuckle
blinds us to an everlasting emptiness
that mortal hunger only echoes. Praise
God for the deserts, famines, droughts with which
he seasons us when we wax fat. And bless
these vacant words as well. Inhabit them."

Spring Cleaning

Mrs. O'Finnicky flounces her dust
ruffles, her mind bent on spring. All winter
she has endured the turgid company
of tchotchkes and assorted bric-a-brac,
of knickknacks worn by constant polishing
until her very need to keep them fresh
has left them faded as her own spent cells;
and yet these souvenirs remind her less
of anything she was than what she's not.
She cleans a reproduction from the Met
of an Egyptian hippopotamus,
then lifts a terra-cotta camel sent
by a daughter on a Middle Eastern tour—
how many years ago? Dust clings to it
as though it still lived on the *badiya*.
She pauses, briefly, fancying herself
a nomad, wandering across a plain
of twisted outcroppings of sun-bleached rock.
She feels a sudden faint, sweet twinge of thirst.
An empty water skin slaps at her thigh.
But somewhere on ahead the lush pastels
of a greeting card mark what ought to be
a palpable oasis, so she goads
her camel through the maze of monuments,
on toward the verdant show. And there she finds
only a canyon's vertical, blank walls
to echo back her emptiness. She counts
the years since either daughter visited.
She thought she had outgrown that loss. But still
her reverie wells up like a bruise: how
she'd fete them with corn-fed, yearling calf, spring
chicken, camel's milk koumiss, the thick fat
dripping and crackling on her heart's banked coals.

Song of Myself

I am a stubborn ox dreaming
of rain as the drover's fingers drum
around my eyes. But no: The wet
hum of flies distracted me,
and now the plow has drifted from
the line I meant to follow. See
where the damp leather of the reins
has worn the callus on my left
forefinger raw? Or was it the dry
ash handle of my hoe? I can hear
the steel head singing as it strikes
rocky ground, the fresh-turned earth
swallowing showers of sparks. The tip
of my tongue goes dry. I touch my lips
to the soil as I once touched you, here
and there. A single knot of dirt
crumbles slowly in my mouth
with the taste of sweet butter dripping
from your thumb. This ground will raise
a heavy crop. I am the wheat
that flowed around your waist like water.
I am that lonely knot of earth.

New England Ghazal

In the beginning were the Words of God, disguised as stones:
like hard, black pupils dropped into the faithful's eyes, these
    stones.

Waves hunched in worship shake the granite shore beneath my
    feet
as once it shuddered under the soles that colonized these stones.

Salt of the earth, they said, "Let nothing grow upon this spot
till Hell silts over. Let them lie among blowflies and stones."

No schist for me, no strata resurrected from dead tongues.
I'll cleave to coal and shale and strive to anglicize the stones.

Cursing a blue streak when his plow beached on a granite spur,
the farmer wiped his brow, letting his sweat baptize these stones.

"Fuck you, you fucking fucker," froths a four foot grade-school
    kid,
thrilled to outdo his friends, who've grown curt, coarse, street-
    wise, like stones.

Praise limestone. Mouth a marble chip. Haunt dikes, tors, sills,
    and crags.
In drought, clay sheathes its softer self and identifies with stones.

Such meditation on the inner life: the CAT scan's Ommm;
unearthly images of what metastasized as stones.

Who doesn't long to blame someone for our infirmities?
I turn to God and nature, but their alibis are stones.

The Jackal sings his privy business to the world at large.
Hungry, unfit to kill, he grumbles lullabies to stones.

Notes

"Entrée": Ralph and Bill refer to Ralph Waldo Emerson and William Blake, specifically to Emerson's *Nature:* "I become a transparent eyeball; I am nothing; I see all"; and Blake's "A Vision of The Last Judgment": "I question not my Corporeal or Vegetative Eye any more than I would Question a Window concerning a Sight I look thro it & not with it."

"The Ninth Month" is for HMKH. The phrase "This is the book in which there is no doubt" occurs in the second sura of the Qur'an.

"A True Story" is for Betsy. For "tranquil recollections" and half-remembering, see William Wordsworth, "Preface to the Second Edition of *Lyrical Ballads*" and "Lines Composed a Few Miles Above Tintern Abbey."

"Sheikh Majnoon": Ben Sikran is an indigent rascal and student in North African Arab folktales.

"Shit" is for Derek. The CDC is the Center for Disease Control and Prevention. Saffra is a brand of bottled water. Parts of section 5 echo Matthew Arnold's "Dover Beach." Section 9 makes use of Emily Dickinson's "After great pain, a formal feeling comes" (#341).

"Impostors" is for Shahid. The epigraph is my translation of the final lines of Canto XXIX of *The Inferno,* which describes the Falsifiers. Moses carried a staff shaped like a coiled serpent. Mount Nebo is where he looked into the Promised Land and died.

"The Invisible World" is for Daniel. The opening echoes Keats's "Fancy."

"The Hospitality of Sheikh Majnoon" plays host to Robert Frost, "The Silken Tent," Wallace Stevens, "Anecdote of the Jar," and Elizabeth Bishop, "Filling Station."

"The Empty Quarter" is for Thomas. "Rub 'al Khali" means the "Quarter of Emptiness"—an uninhabitable part of the desert.

"The House of God": Deir Allah, in the Jordan Valley, is known as the site of Jacob's vision of the ladder of angels. The name means "House of God." The story of Jacob, including his vision, his pillow stone, his angelic wrestling match, and his bowl of porridge (or pottage, depending on the translation), is told in Genesis 25–35. There is a kind of phlox called Jacob's ladder.

"Sheikh Majnoon in Mufti" is for Mark.

Glossary

Ahlain: Welcome.

Arabee: Arabic.

badiya: badlands.

beit shaar: goat hair tents used by the Bedouin.

djinni (pl. **djinn**): a magical being of great power capable of assuming human or animal form.

duri: straight.

fellah (pl. **fellahin**): a farmer, as opposed to a Bedouin, or nomad.

fouwara: a fountain outside a mosque that provides water for cleaning the hands, feet, and face before prayer.

ghoul (pl. **ghoulem**): a demon or evil spirit that feeds on corpses.

habibi: darling.

Hamdullilah: Thanks be to God.

imam: a Muslim prayer leader and scholar.

kaffiyeh: a cloth headdress worn by Arab men.

Keyf ha lak (fem. *Key'fik*): How are you?

koumiss: the fermented milk of a mare or camel.

Ma'andeesh mehni: I don't mind.

majnoon: a fool.

Marhaba: Hello.

masbaha: a string of Muslim prayer beads.

mensaf: a large platter of rice topped with mutton or beef that has been cooked in yogurt with almonds or pine nuts; it is often served to honor a guest.

muezzin: a Muslim crier responsible for calling the faithful to prayer; the call itself is often taped and played over a loudspeaker.

mufti: civilian clothes worn by someone who usually dresses in a uniform.

Ramadan: the ninth month of the Islamic year, during which the faithful fast each day from sunrise to sunset.

Saba al khair: Good morning.

Salaam alicum: Peace be with you.

schmall: to the left.

sheikh: an honorific title; the leader of an Arab village or extended family.

souk: the old commercial neighborhood in an Arab city.

thawb: a long-sleeved, close-fitting robe usually worn under a looser outer robe.

yameen: to the right.